THE RECORD OF A

FALLEN VAMPIRE

Night is a mysterious time. When the lights are out, I always feel as though things are lurking in the shadows. Thank you for giving me the chance to draw a story about vampires, which dwell in that night. I hope I can capture their anxieties and solitude, as they lurk there in the darkness. –*Yuri Kimura*

Artist Yuri Kimura debuted two short stories in Japan's *Gangan Powered* after winning the Enix Manga Award. Shortly thereafter, she began *The Record of a Fallen Vampire*, which was serialized in Japan's *Monthly Shonen Gangan* through March 2007.

Author Kyo Shirodaira is from Nara prefecture. In addition to *The Record of a Fallen Vampire*, Shirodaira has scripted the manga *Spiral: The Bonds of Reasoning*. Shirodaira's novel *Meitantei ni Hana wo* was nominated for the 8th Annual Ayukawa Tetsuya Award in 1997.

THE RECORD OF A FALLEN VAMPIRE

STORY BY: KYO SHIRODAIRA ART BY: YURI KIMURA

1

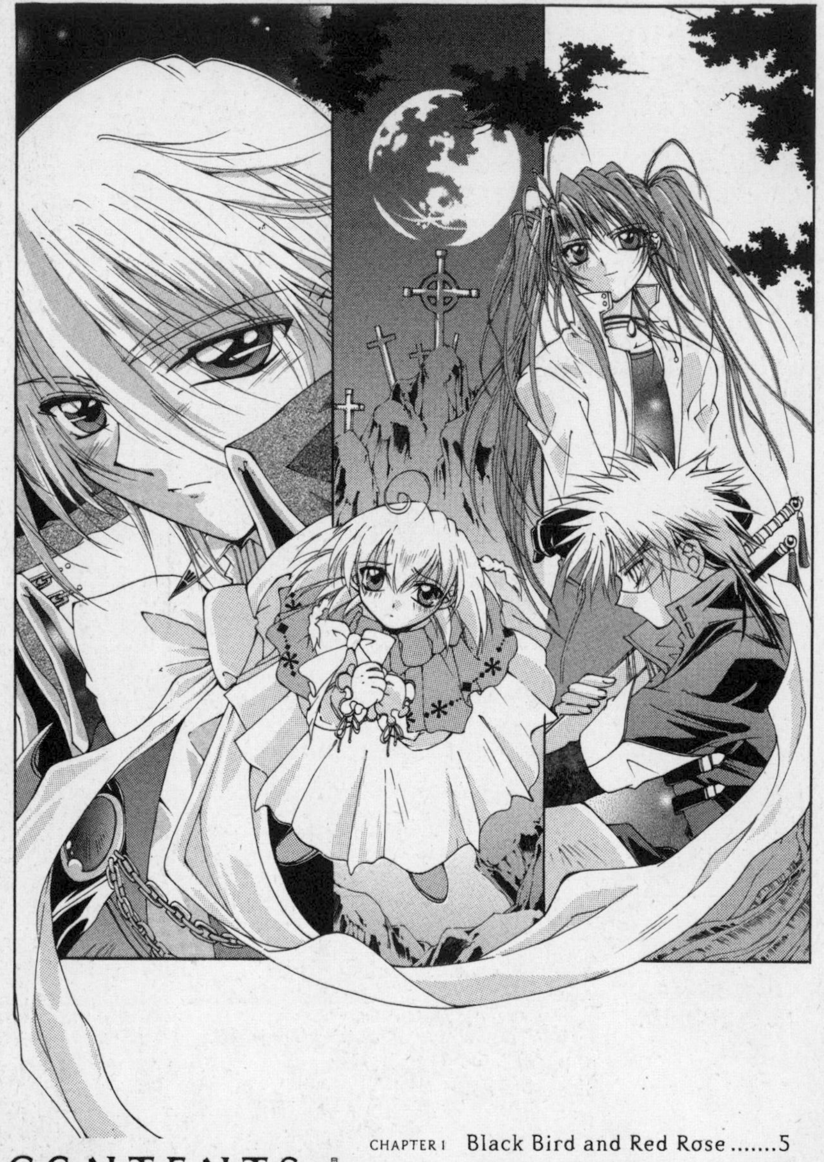

CONTENTS

Chapter 1:
Black Bird
and Red Rose
YOUNG VAMPIRE KING...
YOU HAVE... NO CHANCE... YOU WILL PERISH...
SHING

SKRNCH

Chapter 1:
Black Bird and Red Rose

CLIK
KNGH NGH
DOESN'T MATTER HOW STRONG YOU ARE... THOSE HUMANS WITH VAMPIRE BLOOD...
THOSE *DHAMPIRES* ARE AFTER YOU...
THEY HAVE BOTH MAGIC AND SPIRIT POWERS, ENOUGH TO FIGHT YOU...

AND EVEN... IF YOU KILL ALL THE DHAMPIRES...
THERE'S STILL THE BLACK SWAN...!
KRK
HUMANS POSSESSED BY THE BLACK SWAN...
...WILL PURSUE YOU TILL THE END OF TIME!
YOU WILL FALL!
YOU WILL NEVER... SEE THE CORROSIVE MOONLIGHT AGAIN!
YES... YOU WILL NEVER...
HEHHEHHEHHEHHEH

I WILL GET HER BACK. NO MATTER WHO TRIES TO STOP ME.

FOOOM
NO MATTER HOW LONG IT TAKES.
NO MATTER WHAT I HAVE TO SACRIFICE.
I WILL SEE MY QUEEN ADELHEID AGAIN!!
WHOOM

AND TIME DID PASS...

VOOM
SPLSH
SPLSH SPLSH
VIBRATE EDGE!
SCHIING

FF
FFFF
HAAH!
KIIIIIIIIIING

CLAAAAAAAANG
RRAAA-AAGHH!
KI KIII KIIII
FFAH!
SCHIIIING
SWISH
FWIIIIIIIIP

SWORDS THAT CAN WITHSTAND MY MAGIC? WHEN DID YOU GET THOSE...
...JIN RENKA?
HYUUU

THESE ARE THE SPIRIT SWORDS KORYU AND KINYO. EACH ABSORBED THE SPIRITUAL ENERGY OF THE AIR AND THE EARTH ON A SACRED MOUNTAIN FOR 200 YEARS.
THEY WILL NOT BREAK EASILY, NOT EVEN BEFORE *YOUR* VAST MAGICAL POWER... AKABARA.
YOU CAN IMPROVE YOUR SKILLS AND YOUR WEAPONS, BUT YOU ARE A MERE DHAMPIRE. HALF MAN, HALF VAMPIRE.
YOU CANNOT DEFEAT ME.
WHOOSH
SILENCE!! I HAVE TRAINED FOR 400 YEARS TO DEFEAT YOU!
THAT WAS NOT IN VAIN!
LUNGE

KLANG
RENKA, I BECAME KING OF ALL VAMPIRES WHEN I WAS ONLY 200 YEARS OLD...
ALL THE OTHER VAMPIRES FEARED ME. DO YOU THINK I CAN BE DEFEATED SO EASILY?
SCHIIING
UNGH...

VIBRATE ARROW!
SHA
SHA
SHA
HMPH
WHAT OF IT?
VSH
SWORD!

OBEY THE SPIRITS
WITHIN ME!
WHOOOOM
HAAAAAH!
SCK
WOOOOSH

ZING
ZING
VOOOOORRR
I'M NOT FINISHED YET!
SSHH SHH
TURN, KORYU!
ZZZZT
STRIKE THE RED ROSE!
VWIP VWIP
!
VWIP
VWIP VWIP
VWIP

ROOOOOOOAAAAR
SIGH...
VVVOT
SCHIING
FUTILE!

CHING
MMM!
SSHA
CHING
TODAY IS YOUR END!!
RRROO
OOOOARR

DOFFFFF
THAT WON'T WORK, RENKA.
CLAAAAANG
ARGH!
GRAB

WO
M
NGH
CURSE YOU...!
VIBRATE EDGE!

BOOM
KRK
AAAAAUGHHHH!
SHHUUUUU
GRAB

FOOOOOOM
SWISH
FWASH
FWASH
...
SPLASH
FYUUU

ESCAPED AGAIN...

SIGH

THAT DHAMPIRE ALWAYS SURVIVES.

SSHHHH

WOOSH

SSHHHH
SSHH
SSHH
RENKA AND THE OTHER DHAMPIRES ARE GETTING STRONGER...
IT'S GETTING TO BE A PROBLEM.
AND THEN THERE'S THE BLACK SWAN...
SHH SHHH
HOW LONG WILL I BE ABLE TO STOP HER?
HEY! YOU THERE!

WAGGLE
GOT A LIGHT?
...A LIGHT?
NO...
AH WELL.
Mm...
GRAB

FSSHH
FFF...
I'M ALMOST OUT OF OIL. THERE'S NOWHERE AROUND TO GET MORE...
THOUGHT I'D TRY AND SAVE IT.
WHAT BRINGS YOU HERE?
I MIGHT ASK YOU THE SAME.
SS
BUSINESS.

THERE'S A BIG ISLAND ABOUT TWO KILOMETERS OUT TO SEA.
THEY SAY A VAMPIRE QUEEN HAS BEEN SEALED AWAY THERE.
APPARENTLY, THIS QUEEN'S MAGIC WENT OUT OF CON-TROL AND SHE ALMOST DESTROYED THE WORLD.
SO THE HUMANS TRIED TO KILL HER, BUT...
...SHE WAS TOO STRONG. ALL THEY COULD DO WAS SEAL HER AWAY.
AND THEY SAY THAT WHEN HUMANS HAVE THE POWER TO KILL HER...
...THE SEAL WILL BREAK, AND THEY CAN FINISH HER OFF.
FLICK

BUT THERE ARE OVER A THOUSAND PLACES ALL OVER THE WORLD...
...WHERE THE QUEEN IS SUPPOSED TO BE SEALED.
THE VAMPIRE KING IS TRYING TO FIND HER...
...BEFORE THE HUMANS DESTROY HER.
ACTUALLY, THE HUMANS MADE THOUSANDS OF FAKE SEALS TO FOOL THE KING AND KEEP HIM FROM HER.
EVEN THE HUMANS THEMSELVES NO LONGER KNOW WHICH ONE IS THE REAL THING.
THE KING IS BREAKING THE SEALS ONE BY ONE, ENDLESSLY SEARCHING FOR HER...
...EVEN THOUGH SHE WILL TRY TO DESTROY THE WORLD AGAIN.
ONE THOUSAND YEARS HAVE PASSED, AND STILL THE QUEEN IS SEALED.
STILL THE KING SEARCHES FOR HER...
...FIGHTING THE HUMANS AND DHAMPIRES THAT WOULD KILL HIM AND HIS QUEEN.

AREN'T YOU GETTING TIRED, AKABARA STRAUSS?
THE "RED ROSE" VAMPIRE KING!
SO YOU'RE THE NEW BLACK SWAN?
FLAP
EXACTLY! THE 49TH BLACK SWAN, YUKI KOMATSUBARA.
GRIN
MORTAL ENEMY OF YOU AND THE QUEEN.

FLAP
CHECKED THE SEAL ON THE ISLAND YET?
SCRUNCH
APPARENTLY IT REQUIRES VERY POWERFUL MAGIC TO BREAK.
ASIDE FROM RENKA, YOU'VE BEATEN THE CRAP OUT OF ALL THE DHAMPIRES. THEY CAN'T STOP YOU.
HMMM
OH? THEN I SHOULD BEAT YOU NOW AND DESTROY THE SEAL AS WELL.
YEAH, YEAH. I'VE BEEN FORCED INTO THIS STUPID FIGHT AGAINST MY WILL...
...SO DO ME A FAVOR AND DIE QUIETLY?
NEVER!!
SSHA
SSHA
FLICK

FZZZ
CATCH
YOU DIDN'T FORGET, DID YOU? I CAN NEGATE ALL MAGIC...
WITH THE BLACK SWAN'S ARMS!
SHE NEGATED VIBRATE ARROW ALMOST COMPLETELY...
I CAUSED A BIT OF DAMAGE TO THE BLACK SWAN BEFORE HER, BUT...

FOOM
FOOM
WHAT'S WRONG, AKABARA? I'M NOT AS WEAK AS MY PREDECESSOR, AM I?
DON'T GET COCKY. ONLY THOSE ARMS ARE IMMUNE TO MAGIC.
THE REST OF YOU MAY HAVE STRONG SPIRIT POWER, BUT YOU'RE ONLY HUMAN.
ALL I HAVE TO DO IS GET A VIBRATE ARROW PAST YOUR ARMS!
VVVVVV
FFFF...
CAN YOU?

WOOSH

VIBRATE BLADE!!
SCRUNCH
FOOM
SHE'S FAST!
DSHHHH
...AND ACCURATE!
VOOP

VIP VIP
SCHUNK
YOU'RE WIDE OPEN, AKABARA!
UNGH...

SCHING
SCHIIN

FFFF
FFFF

THE BLACK SWAN'S POWER IS FAR STRONGER THAN I EXPECTED...

I'M IN TROUBLE AT THIS RATE...
SQUEEZE

FSH
THE BLACK SWAN GROWS STRONGER WITH EACH GENERATION.
AND WITH MY GENERATION, I HAVE MATCHED YOU!
...

TKK
AH!
OH NO...!
SPIN
FOOOSH
AGH!
SPLSHH

RUMBLE
CHEAP TRICKS, AKABARA?!
W...
SSHHH
TKK
HEY!
OH...
NO NEED TO RUSH. I CAN WAIT FOR HIM AT THE ISLAND...

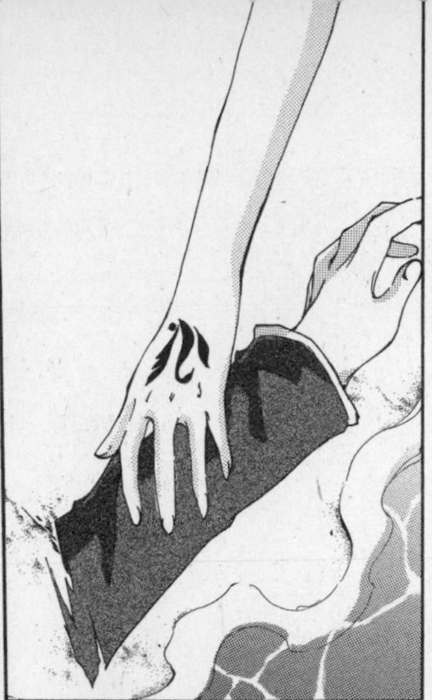

SPLSH

MM?

FLAP
AKABARA?
TWITCH
I WAS ALL NICE AND LET YOU FIGHT HIM ONE ON ONE...AND NOW LOOK AT YOU.

HE LEFT THIS AND RAN.
TOSS
NOT ONE TO HESITATE, IS HE?
HE WON'T GROW THAT BACK IN A HURRY...
HE'S BADLY HURT.

HOW ARE YOU?
SPLASH
IT'LL HEAL BY NIGHT-FALL.
GRRR
I HAVE NO MAGIC OR SPIRIT POWER LEFT, BUT I CAN STILL FIGHT!
SIGH...
GOOD TO KNOW.

...
SPRT
WE SHOULD REACH THE ISLAND BEFORE DAWN.
WAIT FOR AKABARA THERE.

TIKKTKKTKK
TIKK
TIKK

ALMOST DAWN...
HAVE TO FIND SOMEWHERE OUT OF THE SUN BEFORE I TAKE ANY MORE DAMAGE...
RUSTLE
!
VOOOM
AIIIEEEEE!
EEEK!
WOOSH
THUNK
THUD
THUMP
...!!

BOING
OWWW...
I HIT MY NOSE...
A CHILD? THIS DEEP IN THE MOUNTAINS?
TH-THAT WAS MAGIC, WASN'T IT?
BOING
ARE YOU A DHAMPIRE TOO?
BOING
AM I...
...TOO?
AHH!

BAM
WHAT HAPPENED TO YOUR ARM?! CAN YOU GROW IT BACK?
OH, I GET IT...YOU DON'T HAVE MUCH VAMPIRE BLOOD EITHER.
DID THE HUMANS DO THIS?

DON'T WORRY! I DON'T HAVE MUCH VAMPIRE BLOOD, BUT I'M STILL A DHAMPIRE!

YOU'RE SAFE WITH ME!

IT DOESN'T HURT. IT DOESN'T HURT.
LOOKS LIKE SHE'S A STRAY DHAMPIRE... NOTHING TO DO WITH THE BLACK SWAN.

EVEN IF YOUR BLOOD IS THIN, YOU DON'T LIKE THE SUN, RIGHT?
MY HOUSE IS HIDDEN OVER HERE!
YANK
!!
HURRY! HURRY!

♪
♪
♪♫
GLUG
GLUG GLUG

OKAY!
GLEAM

HERE YOU ARE!
GRIN

MY NAME'S LAETITIA.
I'VE BEEN HERE ABOUT FIVE YEARS, AND NOBODY'S FOUND ME.
YOU'LL BE SAFE HERE!

YOU WERE BEING CHASED BY STUPID HUMANS, RIGHT?
GRRRR
THEY'RE SO MEAN!!
HEH...

WHY DO YOU LIVE HERE, LAETITIA?
CLINK

AH
NGH
I CAN'T LIVE WHERE THE HUMANS ARE.
I'M EIGHTEEN, BUT I'M TINY LIKE A CHILD AND NOT GOOD AT MAGIC...
I GROW SLOW, SO I CAN'T STAY IN ONE PLACE TOO LONG.

I'M SO SMALL THEY START SUSPECTIN' SOMETHING REAL QUICK AND SOME-TIMES TRY TO KILL ME.
WHISK
I GOT NO CHOICE BUT TO HIDE.

WHAT ABOUT YOUR PARENTS? ONE OF THEM MUST HAVE VAMPIRE BLOOD...

OH...
MY MOTHER... WAS A DHAMPIRE, BUT THE VILLAGERS FOUND OUT...
THEY CHASED US...
I GOT AWAY.
SORRY. I SHOULDN'T HAVE...
VAMPIRE HUNTING IS STILL GOING ON?
YEAH...
SNIFF
THAT VILLAGE WAS PAR-TICULARLY TERRIFIED.
THEY SAID THAT A LONG TIME AGO A VAMPIRE QUEEN'S CORROSIVE MAGIC ALMOST DESTROYED THE WORLD...
THEY CALLED HER "CORROSIVE MOONLIGHT," CURSING HER NAME...
...

RUMBLE
BUT WHO CARES?!
THAT WAS AGES AGO! NOTHING TO DO WITH ME!
SWISH
I DON'T *WANT* TO FIGHT WITH HUMANS!
AND VAMPIRES AND HUMANS USED TO LIVE TOGETHER PEACEFULLY.
THE VAMPIRES HAD THE KINGDOM OF THE NIGHT, DIDN'T THEY?
YES...
THEY DID.
A KINGDOM OF PEACE, WHERE THE HUMANS WORSHIPED VAMPIRES AS GODS...
AND THE QUEEN RUINED ALL OF THAT! MADE OUR LIVES HORRIBLE!
CLENCH
I JUST... I JUST WANT TO LIVE A QUIET LIFE...

WHY DO VAMPIRES EVEN EXIST?
WHY DID I HAVE TO BE BORN LIKE THIS?
IF I'D NEVER BEEN BORN, I'D NEVER HAVE TO FEEL THIS WAY!
SOME SAY THAT LONG AGO...
THE VAMPIRES CAME FROM BEYOND THE MOON.
EH?
FROM THE MOON?
SMILE
LAETITIA, HAS ANYONE TOLD YOU WHY THE QUEEN ALMOST DESTROYED THE WORLD...
...AND WHY THE KINGDOM OF THE NIGHT MET ITS END?

HUH?
UM...
BECAUSE THE VAMPIRE KING WAS TOO STRONG?
YES... THE KING'S MAGIC WAS MUCH TOO POWERFUL.
HE WAS FEARED NOT ONLY BY HUMANS, BUT BY HIS OWN KIND AS WELL.
THEY WERE SO SCARED THEY TRIED TO KILL HIM.
AND THEY TOOK THE QUEEN HOSTAGE, SO THE KING GAVE HIMSELF UP...
...BUT THE QUEEN TURNED OUT TO BE EVEN STRONGER, RIGHT?
AND SHE TRIED TO TEACH THE REBELS A LESSON WITH THAT POWER...
BUT THE QUEEN HERSELF HAD NO IDEA JUST HOW STRONG HER MAGIC WAS.
AND NO IDEA HOW TO USE THAT POWER...
!!
HALF MAD WITH FEAR THAT THE KING WOULD DIE, HER MAGIC WENT OUT OF CONTROL.

SHE ALMOST DESTROYED THE WORLD AND WAS HEARTLESSLY SEALED AWAY...

FURIOUS, THE KING FOUGHT VAMPIRE AND HUMAN, TRYING TO GET HER BACK...

...AND THE KINGDOM OF THE NIGHT WAS DESTROYED.

SO DON'T BE TOO HARD ON THE QUEEN. IT'S ALL THE KING'S FAULT.

STROKE

HE COULDN'T PROTECT HIS QUEEN...

...OR HIS COUNTRY.

BEING A VAMPIRE IS NOT A BAD THING. IT WAS THE KING WHO RUINED EVERY-THING...

THEY WERE CHASING YOU... YOU HAVE NOWHERE TO GO, RIGHT?
THEN... WHY NOT STAY HERE?
GRAB
I'M SO LONELY...
I CAN'T STAND IT ANYMORE...
SQUEEZE

WILL I EVER BE ABLE TO PAY FOR MY SINS?
THIS CHILD IS ANOTHER OF MY VICTIMS ...
EVEN THE BLACK SWAN...
VICTIMS...
VISH
EVERYONE WHO'S CHASING ME...
THEY ARE MY VICTIMS TOO...
KEE

HEY.
MM?
I'VE MET A NUMBER OF WOMEN THAT WERE POSSESSED BY THE BLACK SWAN...
BUT YOU'RE DIFFERENT.
YEAH!!
JUDGING FROM THE MEMORIES I RECEIVED, THE OTHERS WERE ALL SORT OF TRAGIC, RIGHT?
SSH
THE BLACK SWAN'S A SPIRITUAL PARASITE.
IT POSSESSES HUMANS WITH STRONG SPIRIT POWERS AND GIVES THEM ARMS THAT CAN KILL THE VAMPIRE KING.
CLNK
WHEN ITS HOST DIES, IT FINDS A NEW ONE, GIVING THE NEW HOST ALL THE MEMORIES, ABILITIES, AND SKILLS OF ITS PREDECESSORS...
...AND MAKES THEIR PHYSICAL ABILITIES SUPERHUMAN.
IN OTHER WORDS, THE BLACK SWAN GETS STRONGER WITH EACH GENERATION.
...

IF YOU DON'T KILL THE VAMPIRE KING WITHIN FIVE YEARS, THE BLACK SWAN EATS ITS HOST...
THEN IT SEARCHES FOR A NEW HOST, DELIBERATELY SPEEDING UP THE CYCLE.
STAND
YOU DIE EITHER WAY, SO I CAN SEE WHY THEY WERE KINDA TRAGIC.
LIKE YOU'RE SOME SORT OF HUMAN SACRIFICE...
THE BLACK SWAN IS A MYSTIC FORCE, ABLE TO BUILD POWER WITHOUT LIMIT IN ORDER TO KILL THE VAMPIRE KING.
THE MOST POWERFUL CURSE THE HUMANS EVER UNLEASHED ON THE WORLD.
IF AKABARA WERE GONE, YOU'D HAVE...
OW!
THOK
ZA ZA ZAZA
ZA ZA ZA

WHOOM
OOWAHH !!
DON'T TALK LIKE THAT. SURE, I'M A LITTLE PISSED...
BUT THERE'S SOMETHING TO BE SAID FOR A SHORT LIFE FILLED WITH EXCITEMENT.
YOU...
HUF
I DON'T CARE ABOUT THE BLACK SWAN!
I JUST DON'T...
I DON'T WANT YOU TO...
WAG

REMEMBER, I MIGHT NOT DIE.
DROP
IF I KILL AKABARA AND THE CORROSIVE MOONLIGHT BEFORE MY TIME LIMIT, THE BLACK SWAN'LL VANISH.
AND I CAN GO BACK TO MY OLD LIFE.
YUKI...
FFF
IT'S NOT SO BAD.
I HAVE SOMEONE WHO CARES THIS MUCH FOR ME...
WHO'S WILLING TO GO THROUGH IT ALL WITH ME...
THE STRENGTH OF THE BLACK SWAN OF MY GENERATION HAS MATCHED THE VAMPIRE KING'S...
I WILL DEFEAT THE RED ROSE...

WAIT!

TUG

TUG

WHERE ARE YOU GOING?

ARE YOU GOING TO LEAVE ME ALONE AGAIN?

I'M SORRY. THERE'S SOMETHING I HAVE TO DO.
NO MATTER WHAT HAPPENS TO ME...
NO! WE ONLY JUST MET!
I KNOW SOMEONE WHO IS ESTABLISHING A DHAMPIRE COMMUNITY... YOU WON'T BE LONELY THERE.
I'LL SEND SOMEONE TO GET YOU TOMORROW.
TUSSLE
BUT...
MAY THE GRACE OF THE MOON BE WITH THEE...

FAREWELL, LAETITIA ...
FLAP
FLAP
IS HE ...?
HE MUST BE THE LEGEND-ARY VAMPIRE KING...
...WHO'S BEEN SEARCHING FOR HIS QUEEN FOR A THOUSAND YEARS...

THE RED ROSE APPROACHES.
DON'T TRY TOO HARD. JUST DRIVE HIM ON LAND, AND I'LL DO THE REST.
BLINK
...
I'M A MAN, YOU KNOW. I'LL MAKE THINGS AS EASY FOR YOU AS I CAN.
SHH
...YUKI.
I'VE KNOWN YOU SINCE BEFORE THE BLANK SWAN POSSESSED YOU.
SO...
...I SHOULD SAY THIS NOW.

WHEN ALL THIS IS OVER, WILL YOU BE WITH ME?
I MAY BE A DHAMPIRE, BUT THERE ARE WAYS TO BECOME FULLY HUMAN.
BLUSH
SO IF YOU'D...BE WITH ME...
SH HA
SHHH

...
I'LL THINK ABOUT IT.
TAP
BUT FIRST...
...WE HAVE TO MAKE SURE THIS IS OVER.

WHOOOOSH
VVVVVRRRRRR
CLANG

FOOM
I'VE BEEN WAITING FOR YOU, AKABARA!
...
JIN RENKA.
VVV
I HAVE A FAVOR TO ASK.
WHAT?

IN THE MOUNTAINS TO THE WEST, A LITTLE DHAMPIRE IS HIDING.
TAKE HER TO YOUR COMMUNITY.
HER PARENTS WERE KILLED BY HUMANS, AND SHE HAS NOWHERE ELSE TO GO.
SO WHAT ?!
CLANG
...
FOR ONE THING...
BECAUSE I NEED YOU TO DO THAT...

RRRRRRR
?!
I'LL SPARE YOUR LIFE TODAY!
BOOOM

RRRRRRR
YUKI...
YUKI...!
FOOM
BOOOOOM!!

GLARE
WHERE'S RENKA?
I BURNED AWAY TWO-THIRDS OF HIS BODY. HE SHOULD BE ABLE TO MOVE BY DAWN.
SO NOTHING BUT THESE HANDS CAN DEFEAT YOUR MAGIC.
DEFEATING MY MAGIC DOES NOT MEAN YOU CAN WIN.

WHOOSH
SWISH

VVVV
VIBRATE...
ZK
...CYCLONE!!
OOR
!!
FFF...
RRRR
RRRR
RR

WHAT ARE YOU PLAYING AT, AKABARA?
YOU CAN THROW ALL THE MAGIC AROUND YOU LIKE. AS LONG AS THESE ARMS CAN REACH IT, YOU WON'T HURT ME.
BLINK
RRRRRR
SWOOSH
AH!
ZAZA
!
FFFFFF
I SEE!
MAGIC CAN'T HURT ME DIRECTLY, SO HE'S USING IT TO THROW THINGS AT ME...

HEH
PATHETIC!
VVOORR
CLNK
THE SPIRIT POWER OF ALL THE BLACK SWANS FLOWS THROUGH ME!
RRRRRRR
ONLY A DIRECT MAGICAL ATTACK CAN PENETRATE THIS BARRIER, AKABARA!
I'LL KNOW WHERE YOU ARE ONCE YOU ATTACK...THEN I'LL CLOSE THE GAP INSTANTLY AND END THIS!

KIIIIIIIN
KA
BOOM
NOT THAT EASY!!
SSHHH

KIIII
IT'S OVER, AKABARA!!
IIIING

?!
TOK
THNK
AH...?
DRIP
KORYU AND KINYO ?!
STAGGER
STAGGER
THESE ARE... RENKA'S SWORDS ...
RENKA'S FAVORITE SPIRIT SWORDS.
ABLE TO GET PAST THE BLACK SWAN'S ARMS AND YOUR BARRIER.

OH... BACK WHEN HE...
HE LET THEM RIDE THE WIND...
...HIDDEN BETWEEN HIM AND THE BOULDERS...
VOOM
FOOOOOOM
SSHHH

HOW LAME...
I GOT SO COCKY...
COUGH
SHHHHHH
BUT...THE NEXT BLACK SWAN...THE 50TH...WILL HAVE ALL MY SKILLS, MEMORIES, AND SPIRIT POWER...
THIS WON'T WORK TWICE. SHE'LL BE...EVEN STRONGER THAN ME.

THE NEXT BLACK SWAN... WILL PROBABLY KILL YOU.
FLICK

PERHAPS.
THOUGH IF I WIN, THE NEXT WILL BE EVEN STRONGER.
YOU NEVER GET A BREAK, DO YOU?

CLICK
CLICK
MM?
DANG...
CLICK

OUT OF OIL...
FWSH
!

YOU LIT IT WITH MAGIC?
THANKS.

FFWOO
AH, THAT'S GREAT.
THE STARS ARE SO PRETTY ...
I'M SORRY. THIS IS ALL BECAUSE OF...
STOP IT.
THIS IS ALL FOR THE GIRL YOU LOVE, RIGHT?
NO REASON TO WASTE TIME.
VISH

AKABARA STRAUSS ...
YOU'RE A GOOD GUY. I DON'T HATE YOU FOR THIS. REALLY.
AH...
I NEVER ANSWERED HIM...
REN...
...KA...

SIGH...

FLAP

KRNCH
VVIIING
CLINK
THIS WASN'T IT EITHER...

I HAVE TO GO FIND ANOTHER SEAL...
HAVE TO BREAK IT WITH THESE BLOOD-STAINED HANDS...
AND THEN DO IT AGAIN AND AGAIN, ON AND ON...
AS LONG AS THERE IS A MOON...
AS LONG AS THERE IS NIGHT...
...UNTIL I AM KILLED.

KRNCH

TOTTER

SNAP
STAGGER
UNGH...
UGH...
HAVE TO HURRY...
WHAT HAPPENED TO AKABARA?
DID YUKI...
SHIVER
DID YUKI WIN?
ZAAAA

AAAAUGH!
WHAM
AHH...
AAAHH...
AAAAUGGGH...

PLUP
PLUP
SKRCH
CURSE YOU, AKABARA!
THE BLACK SWAN MAY BE REBORN FOR ALL ETERNITY...
...BUT THE PEOPLE IT POSSESSES ARE NOT IMMORTAL!
YUKI WILL NOT COME BACK!!
KLENCH
YUKI...
YOU DESTROYED YUKI'S LIFE...
IF IT WEREN'T FOR YOU...
...THIS WOULD HAVE NEVER...

AKABARA! I WILL HAVE REVENGE!
I WILL AVENGE YUKI'S DEATH!
NO MATTER WHAT!
FOOOM

Chapter 2:
Wings in Town

THE MAGIC OF THE VAMPIRE QUEEN ADELHEID IS A CORROSIVE MAGIC.

UNLEASHED, IT CORRODES ANYTHING THAT HAS FORM, EVEN LIGHT.
TOTAL ANNIHILATION.

THERE IS NO WAY TO PREVENT IT.
NO POWER THAT *CAN*...
...NOT EVEN SCIENCE.

SNIP
OVER A THOUSAND YEARS AGO, THE QUEEN ALMOST SWALLOWED THE WORLD WITH HER MAGIC.
SHE WAS SEALED AWAY BY HER KIND AND BY HUMANS.
HOWEVER...THE VAMPIRE KING IS TRYING TO DESTROY THAT SEAL IN ORDER TO GET HIS QUEEN BACK.
TO PREVENT THAT FROM HAPPENING, COUNTLESS FAKE SEALS WERE CREATED.
AND THE DHAMPIRES, HUMANS WITH VAMPIRE BLOOD, SEEK TO KILL THE VAMPIRE KING.
SNIP

THE BATTLE STILL RAGES, FROM SEAL TO SEAL.

THE VAMPIRE QUEEN'S MAGIC WAS LIKE A BLACK HOLE OPENING ON THE EARTH.
IF SHE IS RESTORED CARELESSLY, THE WORLD WILL BE DESTROYED?

YES.
SWSH
THE HALF-VAMPIRES... THOSE DHAMPIRES... THEY CANNOT STOP THE QUEEN.
SHHA
THE VAMPIRE KING IS VERY STRONG.
IN TIME, HE WILL FIND THE REAL SEAL AND REVIVE HIS QUEEN.

WHICH IS WHY THE HUMANS CURSED THE KING AND QUEEN WITH ETERNAL DEATH...
SWSH
UNLEASHING A SINGLE BIRD INTO THE WORLD...

THE BLACK SWAN.

KLUNK KLUNK KLUNK
SHHA
STAND
...

TO THINK THAT VAMPIRES REALLY EXIST... THIS, TOO, WAS WRITTEN IN THE STARS.

THE FATE OF HUMANITY RESTS WITH YOU.

DO NOT FAIL THEM, KAYUKI.

I WON'T...
...GRAND-FATHER.
SWISH

SHH
SHHAAA
HYUUUUUU
FLAP
FLAP
FLAP

REMINDS ME...
...OF JUST HOW MUCH THE WORLD HAS CHANGED.

NOTHING LIKE IT A THOUSAND YEARS AGO.
THIS IS AMAZING, STRAUSS!
WE'RE SO HIGH UP!!
KLANG
KLANG
KLANG

BAM
WE'RE ALMOST IN SPACE!!
I CAN ALMOST TOUCH THE MOON!!
ROCKET ROCKET GO GO!!
BOING BOING
...
WOULD YOU LIKE TO?
HUH?

I COULD TAKE YOU THERE, LAETI. A SHORT LITTLE FLIGHT...
WOW! I CAN TELL YOU'RE THE VAMPIRE KING!
FO OM
EVEN YOUR JOKES ARE ON A WHOLE OTHER LEVEL!
ROCKET FEET STRAUSS BOOOOM!
UH...
SHE DOESN'T BELIEVE ME AT ALL...
LIKE I SAID BEFORE...
VAMPIRES ONCE CAME TO EARTH FROM BEYOND THE MOON.
YEP. ♪
SO...
TWIST

AS THE KING OF VAMPIRES, I CAN FLY THERE EASILY.

YEAH, BUT THAT WHOLE BIT ABOUT BEING FROM BEYOND THE MOON...
NOBODY *REALLY* BELIEVES THAT, RIGHT? RIGHT? RIGHT?
THUNK
SLUMP

AFTER ALL, I'M JUST A LOUSY KING WHO LET HIS KING-DOM FALL TO RUIN...
RUMMMMBLE
YEAH
AND IT'S TIME YOU STOPPED BEING GLOOMY ABOUT IT.
SIGH

PERK
FINE, DON'T BELIEVE ME.
TURN

FLAP
THAT'S ENOUGH REST.
I WANT TO FIND ADELHEID'S SEAL AS SOON AS POSSIBLE.
AH! WAIT!
HANG ON!!
SCAN
SCAN
GLINT
BEFORE THE NEW BLACK SWAN APPEARS...
YEAH... THIS TIME...
THIS TIME I HOPE IT'S THE REAL ONE.
WHEN YOU GET ADELHEID BACK, WE SHOULD ALL GO TO THE MOON TOGETHER!!
HM?

OH...
THAT'S NOT A BAD IDEA.
PERHAPS THERE WON'T BE A PLACE FOR US HERE ANY-MORE...

WOOOOOSH

FIFTY YEARS HAVE PASSED SINCE I FIRST MET STRAUSS...

I AM A DHAMPIRE, A HUMAN WITH VAMPIRE BLOOD...

STRAUSS IS A VAMPIRE KING WHO DESTROYED HIS OWN KINGDOM. I JOINED HIM ON HIS JOURNEY TO RECOVER HIS QUEEN.

SHIIIN

OKAY! GOING WELL...

I'M LEARNING A LITTLE MAGIC AND CAN HELP HIM OUT SOMETIMES.

...AH! EH?

FOOSH

WHOA!

YIKES!

THE DHAMPIRES FIGHTING STRAUSS HATE ME FOR IT. OH WELL.

WE'VE DESTROYED A LOT OF SEALS OVER THE LAST FIFTY YEARS, BUT THEY WERE ALL FAKES...

STRAUSS HAS DESTROYED MORE THAN THREE THOUSAND OVER THE LAST MILLENNIUM, BUT HE STILL HASN'T FOUND THE REAL ONE YET.

STRAUSS IS GETTING NERVOUS.
AND WITH GOOD REASON.
THE BLACK SWAN...
HE BEAT THE 49TH ONE FIFTY YEARS AGO, AND THE 50TH STILL HASN'T SHOWN HERSELF...
SHE SHOULD HAVE APPEARED A LONG TIME AGO, BUT FOR NOW, SHE STILL HASN'T...
STRAUSS ISN'T SURE HE CAN BEAT THE 50TH ONE.
...
HE WANTS TO GET THE QUEEN BACK BEFORE SHE APPEARS.
HYUUUU
BUT ALL THE SEALS HE'S BROKEN SO FAR ARE ALL FAKE. HE'S STARTING TO PANIC.
MM?
GRAB

LAETI!
C'mon! Carry me!
THIS IS WHY YOU NEVER GET ANY BETTER!
I don't care! You can take me to the moon!
FFFFFW
WWW
IT'S SO PRETTY...
SO MANY STARS...
IN THE SKY *AND* ON THE GROUND...

SQUEEZE

HOLD ON TIGHT.

HEH HEH...

I HOPE THIS ONE IS THE REAL SEAL.

I HOPE THE BLACK SWAN DOESN'T APPEAR.

Diana flow
Shop
CLICK
FSSHH

...
CHNK
YUKI...
AKABARA KILLED YUKI FIFTY YEARS AGO...AND I STILL HAVEN'T AVENGED HER DEATH.
I'VE FOUGHT AKABARA SO MANY TIMES ALREADY, BUT...
GRIND

AAGH! WHY CAN'T I BEAT HIM?!

ARE VAMPIRES REALLY THAT MUCH MORE POWERFUL THAN DHAMPIRES?!

IS IT IMPOSSIBLE FOR ANYONE TO BEAT HIM EXCEPT THE BLACK SWAN?!
GRP

EVEN HUMANS DON'T WALK AROUND SMOKING ANYMORE.

NOTHING GOOD WILL COME OF OBSESSING OVER AN OLD FLAME.
STEP
JIN RENKA.
HMPH
BRIDGET...
FFF
TELL THAT TO AKABARA.
ANYWAY... YOU SURE YOU'RE RIGHT?
AKABARA'S HEADED FOR THE SEAL AT POINT SEVEN?
NOD
YES.

HE'S IN THE NET... HE'LL BE THERE TONIGHT.
HYUUU
ETHEL AND FUHAKU ARE ALREADY IN POSITION.
THE SEAL IS IN THE CENTER OF TOWN.

I'VE PLACED HYPNOTIC BARRIERS ALL AROUND.
THE AREA 200 METERS AROUND THE SEAL IS AS DESERTED AS POSSIBLE.
REMEMBER THAT WHEN YOU FIGHT.

IT'S NOT LIKE IT USED TO BE. IF WE DESTROY THE HUMANS' BUBBLE, THEY MIGHT START HUNTING VAMPIRES AGAIN.
FUU
DON'T HARM THE TOWN OR THE PEOPLE IN IT.
AKABARA IS MUCH SMARTER ABOUT THAT THAN YOU ARE.

FOLLOW HUMAN RULES! DON'T SHAKE THEIR WORLD!
GRAB
TCH.
VAMPIRE OR DHAMPIRE...
THERE'S NOWHERE LEFT WHERE OUR RULES HOLD SWAY.
THE DAYS WHEN YOU FOUGHT USING BRUTE FORCE IS LONG SINCE GONE.
WHO CARES?
SNAP
WAIT!
HEY! RENKA!
REN...
I JUST...

I JUST WANT TO KILL AKABARA.
THE WORLD AFTER THAT MEANS NOTHING TO ME.
TAP
TAP
FIGURE OUT YOUR OWN VALUE.
TAP
TAP
THERE'S NOTHING SADDER THAN OBSESSING OVER A LOST STAR SO MUCH THAT YOU CAN'T SEE THE NEW ONES.

A LOST STAR?
YEAH...

YOU'LL NEVER REACH A LOST STAR. IF YOU KEEP GAZING AT IT, IT WILL SIMPLY TORTURE YOU.

"RED ROSE" STRAUSS ...WHY DO YOU NOT UNDER-STAND THAT?

THEN AGAIN...
...I'M JUST AS BIG A FOOL.
HYUUUU
I'M STILL ENCHANTED BY THE ROSE...

TARGET ACQUIRED.
BRIDGET'S HYPNOTIC BARRIER...
IT'S WORKING WELL, COVERING ABOUT 200 METERS AROUND.

ENEMIES ARE BRIDGET...
ETHELBERT TAKAHASHI.
...TESSENJI FUHAKU.
AND JIN RENKA.
AN ALL-STAR LINE-UP TONIGHT, ISN'T IT?
HYUUUUU...
YEAH.

THEY KNEW WE WERE COMING... WE MUST HAVE HIT BRIDGET'S NET.
WANNA COME BACK LATER?

WE DON'T HAVE TIME.

STRAUSS IS STRONG ENOUGH TO DESTROY THE ENTIRE AREA WITH ONE BLOW, BUT WE CAN'T DAMAGE THE TOWN...

HE HAS TO FIGHT UP CLOSE, RESTRAIN-ING HIS POWER.

BUT THE GREATER NUMBER HAS THE ADVANTAGE THIS WAY...

DON'T WORRY.
PAT
JUST MAKE SURE THEY DON'T FIND YOU.
...Okay!

THEN...!
FOOM!!
MAY THE GRACE OF THE MOON BE WITH YOU!

YEAH...
AND WITH YOU.
FLAP FLAP FLAP FLAP

GAZE
KA-CHUNK
KIIIIIIIIIING
HYUUUU

!!
THE RED ROSE IS HERE!
NORTH, NORTHEAST. IN THE AIR, 400 METERS AND CLOSING! ALONE!
SWISH
!!
CLANK
AND THE MOUNTAIN CAT?
CLANK
NOT WITHIN 700 METERS.
KEEP LOOKING. SHE MAY NOT HAVE MUCH MAGIC, BUT YOU CAN NEVER TELL WHAT SHE'LL DO...
TKK
TKK
TKK

I'LL TAKE HER OUT AS SOON AS I FIND HER.
OH, AND...
RENKA! PLEASE! DON'T GO ON A RAMPAGE!
TRY AND STOP ME.
I'LL KILL HIM WHEN I GET THE SLIGHTEST CHANCE.
TCH
NO MATTER WHAT!!

FOOOM
WOOOSH
...
FINE!!
JUST BEAT AKABARA TO THE GROUND!
HE HAS THE ADVANTAGE IN THE AIR!!
OOOOOOO
GRIND
ZZZZZT
ZT

ZZZZZZZT

FOOSH
WHOOM
AKABARA...
I WILL CRUCIFY YOU... THE WAY YOU DID YUKI!
KIIIIII

THWAK
CLANG
AKABARARAAAAA!
WRRRR
WRRR
WRRRRRRRRR

SIGH
DON
DON
FOOOOM

FOOM
RRAAAAAGH!!
PUTT
GRRR...
SH
ARGH...
IF I OUTPUT MORE MAGIC, I CAN FLING HIM ASIDE EASILY... BUT THAT WOULD DAMAGE THE AREA.
THAT MAKES THINGS HARD...
WH
...!!
WOOM

...
STRAUSS IS HOLDING BACK, TRYING NOT TO DAMAGE THE TOWN... BUT WE STILL CAN'T TOUCH HIM.
RENKA AND THE OTHERS HAVE HONED THEIR SKILLS FOR HUNDREDS OF YEARS...
AND WE'RE STILL NO MATCH FOR THE KING?

CLANG
VVV
SPIRIT POWER!
FOOO
KORYU...
KINYO...
YUKI...
GRANT MY HANDS POWER!!
OM

GIVE ME THE STRENGTH...
THE STRENGTH TO SLAY AKABARA !!
GLEEM
HERE WE GO!!
ZAKIIIN
YUKI!!
KIIIIN
IIIN

DON'T RUN AWAY, AKABARAAAA!
GLANCE
RENKA HAS NO INTENTION OF STOPPING...
FOOOOOM
IF I DODGE, HE'LL CRASH THROUGH THE BUILD-ING BEHIND ME...
FLAP
I HAVE TO TAKE IT!

BOOOOM
I'VE BEEN WAITING FOR THIS FOR SO LONG...
THIS MOMENT ...

HAHH
I'VE BEEN WAITING TO DO THIS TO YOU...
TO KILL YOU WITH THE SWORDS YOU USED TO KILL YUKI!
HAHH
LET ME HEAR YOU CRY, AKABARA !!

RENKA... I DO NOT DENY YOUR GRUDGE.
I ADMIT MY OWN SIN.
GRAB
BUT NO MATTER HOW POWERFUL YOUR SPIRIT SWORDS ARE, A SIMPLE STABBING WILL NOT KILL ME.
PAT
YOUR HATRED WEAKENS YOUR ATTACK.
FFF
I'LL BREAK YOUR HANDS BEFORE THE SWORDS MOVE.
FF
GO AHEAD! YOU CAN'T TAKE YOUR HANDS OFF OF MINE...
'CAUSE THE MOMENT YOU DO, I'LL SLICE YOU TO PIECES!!
GGAHH
VA
I'VE GOT ENOUGH SPIRIT POWER IN MY HANDS TO RESIST YOUR MAGIC FOR TEN FULL SECONDS.
VA VA VA

AND DON'T FORGET!
YOU STILL HAVE FUHAKU AND ETHEL TO FIGHT!!
FUHAKU! ETHEL! KILL HIM!!
GO AHEAD!
IF RENKA'S IN YOUR WAY, THEN GO THROUGH HIM!
KILL BOTH OF US!

RENKA! YOU MEAN TO DIE WITH HIM?!
TALK ABOUT SELF-ABSORBED ...
RENKA WAS COUNTING-ING ON THIS...
I'M NOT SURE ABOUT ETHEL, BUT FUHAKU WON'T HESITATE TO KILL RENKA!
KK

BA
AAAM
WH...?!
HSSSSS
NO...
MOUNTAIN CAT?!
!!
SCOWL

BOING
POW!
STRAUSS CHARGED THE BULLETS FULL OF MAGIC SO THEY'RE EXTRA STRONG!
IMPOSSIBLE! I DIDN'T EVEN SMELL HER, MUCH LESS SEE HER!
HOW CAN SHE AIM AT RENKA'S HANDS FROM OVER 700 METERS AWAY?!
GLARE
THEY'RE ALL DISTRACTED!
NOW'S YOUR CHANCE, STRAUSS!!

BOOM
SPLURT
KKAAGH!
WHOOM
AHH!
!!

TKK TKK
TKK
AUGH!
HOW PATHETIC !!

KIIIIIN
JUST HAVE TO BREAK THAT SEAL...
CHASAAA
VIBRATE EDGE!

TOO LATE!
PRAY IT'S NOT REAL...!
...!!
IF THIS IS THE REAL ONE, THE SEAL WILL BREAK...
...AND I CAN GET ADELHEID BACK BEFORE THE 50TH BLACK SWAN APPEARS!
GOOOOO!!

?!
FIZZ

FFFFF
MY MAGIC FIZZLED OUT?
THE ONLY THING THAT CAN DO THAT IS...!
OH NO...

FFFF...

GREETINGS, VAMPIRE KING.
I AM KAYUKI HIRASAKA.
SSHHH
VISH

THE 50TH BLACK SWAN...
THE BIRD OF DESPAIR THAT BRINGS YOU DEATH.

Chapter 3: Yomotsu Hirasaka

I AM KAYUKI HIRASAKA, THE 50TH BLACK SWAN.
THE BIRD OF DESPAIR THAT BRINGS YOU DEATH.

SHUUUU
STAGGER
AT LAST YOU SHOW YOUR-SELF...
...BLACK SWAN!!

THE MAGICAL KILLING BIRD THAT CAN DESTROY ANY FORM OF MAGIC.
OCCASION-ALLY IT HAS TROUBLE FINDING ITSELF A NEW HOST...
BUT AFTER FIFTY YEARS, IT APPEARS AGAIN AT LAST!

THE PREVIOUS BLACK SWAN WAS AKABARA'S EQUAL...
SO THIS BLACK SWAN SHOULD SURPASS HIM!!
NO MATTER HOW POWERFUL AKABARA IS...
THIS TIME...
WE CAN FINISH THINGS!

CLNK
BLACK SWAN...
THE 50TH ...!
WHOOOOO

FROWN
...
WHY THE MASK, BLACK SWAN?
PLEASE IGNORE IT. I AM MERELY A BASHFUL MAIDEN.
?!!

A QUIET, SOUNDLESS GUARD.
NOT A GAP IN HER DEFENSES...

AUGH...

I CAN'T! IF I SHOOT NOW, IT MIGHT MESS UP STRAUSS!
I CAN'T BACK HIM UP AT ALL!
WHAT SHOULD I DO?
NGH NGH

WHAT SHOULD I...?!
WHOO
OOOO
WHAT SHOULD WE DO, BRIDGET ?
DON'T MOVE.

OOO

YOU'LL JUST GET YOURSELF HURT.
HE'S AIMING FOR A FATAL BLOW...
THE AIR IS SHIMMERING WITH MAGIC AND AGGRESSION...

WHOOOO

BUT THE BLACK SWAN IS UTTERLY QUIET...
...WHICH MAKES HER ALL THE MORE SINISTER!

IS SHE THAT MUCH MORE POWERFUL?

TO DEFEAT THE BLACK SWAN, I HAVE TO GET PAST HER ARMS...
CAN'T DO THAT WITH TECHNIQUE, BUT WITH SPEED...
HUF
VSH
HAVE TO MOVE FASTER THAN SHE CAN!

AND TAKE HER DOWN!
WHOOOM
HAH
KRAKL
FOOM
FOOM
FOOM
FOOM

TKK
WHOOOOO

KAFF

FOOOOOM

URNGH...

UNGH...

...

70 PERCENT OF MY ORGANS DESTROYED ...

KOFF KOFF

INJURIES FROM THE BLACK SWAN'S ARMS HEAL SLOWLY...

KOFF

IF YOU CANNOT STAND, THEN TAKE MY HAND.

SHH

...
AKABARA WAS CERTAINLY NOT AT AN ADVANTAGE...
BUT FOR HER TO WIN THAT EASILY...

THE BLACK SWAN REALLY IS...
...AN ETERNALLY INESCAPABLE CURSE!
THIS FEELS ANTICLIMATIC AFTER OUR THOUSAND YEARS OF BATTLE...
BUT AT LAST...
...AKABARA IS FINISHED.
BAAAAANG
...?!

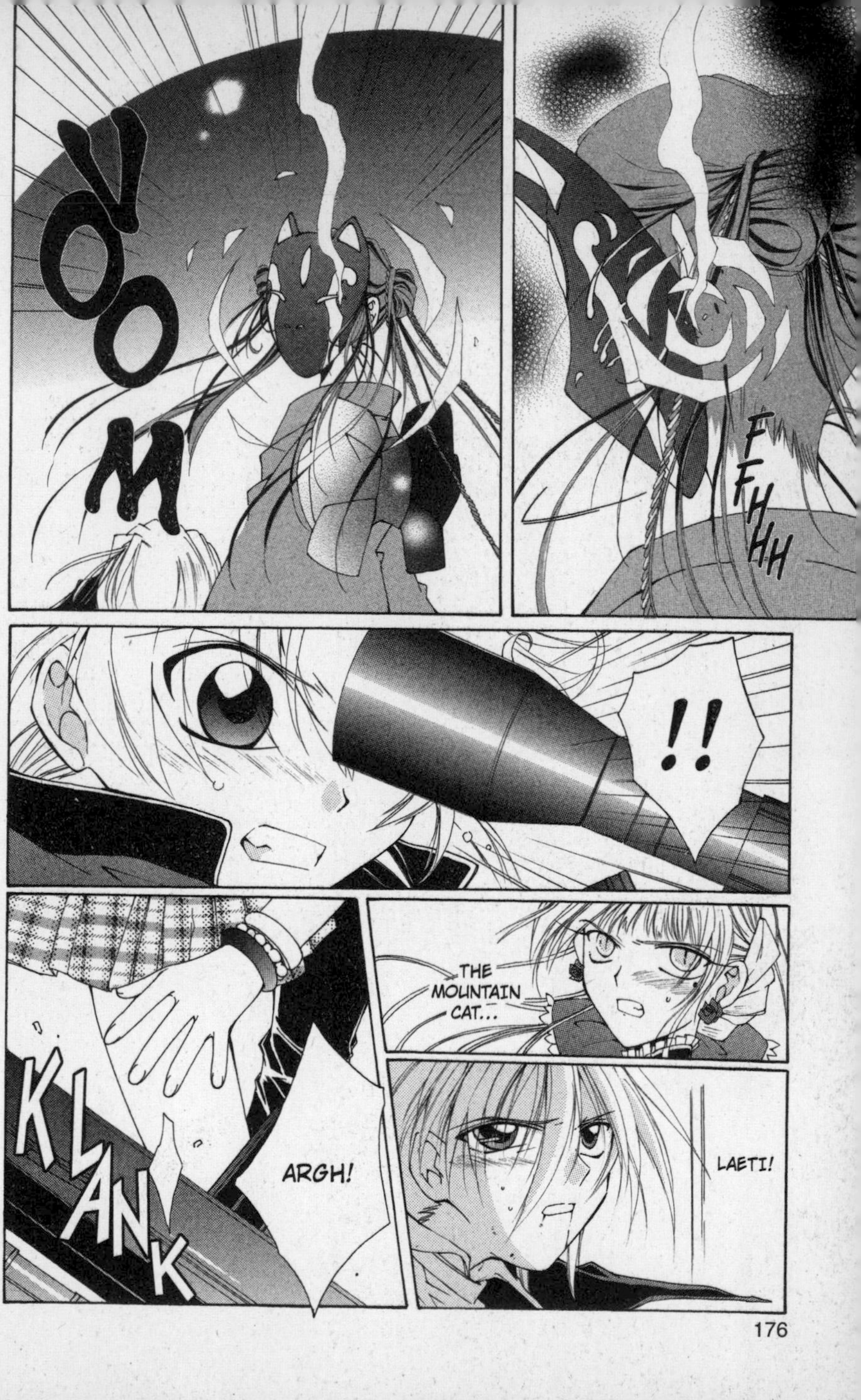

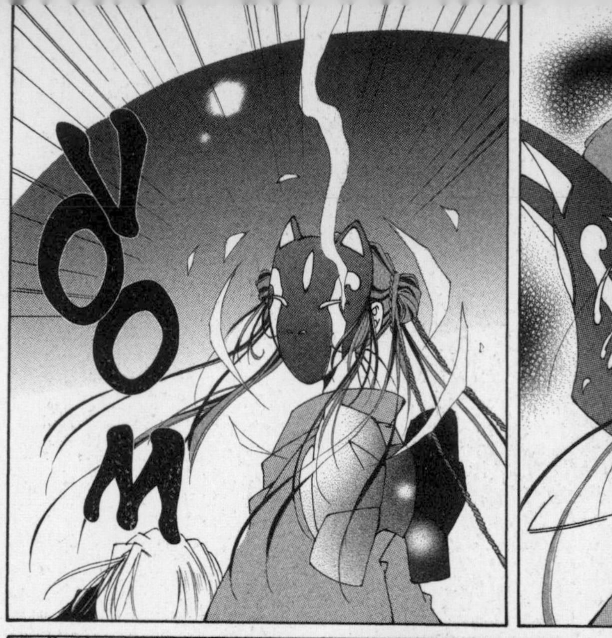

!!

THE MOUNTAIN CAT...

KLANK

ARGH!

LAETI!

I'M TOO FAR AWAY!!
YANK
YANK
CHNK
COME ON... GOT IT!
BOUND
I HAVE TO HURRY !!
AH!
GASP
OOPS
WHOOOOSH
AUGGGGGHHH!

BUMP
ACK!
SPLAT
AUGH!!
VSH
STUPID!
THIS IS *NOT* THE TIME TO FALL!
I HAVE TO SAVE HIM...
I HAVE TO HURRY!
VOORR
CONCENTRATE! CONCENTRATE!
NOW...
I'M COMING...!

STRAUSS!!

WHO IS THAT?

IT SEEMS YOU HAVE A FRIEND?

KILLING ME IS ENOUGH, ISN'T IT?

PLEASE DON'T HURT HER.

NUMBER 50...
ALLOW ME TO STRIKE THE FINAL BLOW.
YOU MUST HAVE... YUKI'S MEMORIES.
YOU KNOW WHY I ASK THIS.
CHNK
TKK

TKK
TKK
ON THAT DAY...
...YOU PIERCED YUKI WITH THESE SWORDS...
GRIP
AKABARA...
NOW THEY WILL CARVE YOUR BODY!!
TKK
SWISH

AKABARA... FALLEN VAMPIRE KING...
THIS IS YOUR FUNERAL SWORD.
IT WILL EXACT PAYMENT FOR YOUR SINS UNTIL YOUR FLESH CAN TAKE NO MORE!
CHNK

YUKI...

WHY COULDN'T I...

...PROTECT YOU?

TUMP
WHAM
WH...
WHAT ...?!
GASP

THE BLACK SWAN DEFENDED AKABARA?!
GRR
FOOM
PROTECTING THE VAMPIRE KING.
WHAT ARE YOU DOING, BLACK SWAN?!
YOU WANT TO FINISH HIM YOUR-SELF?
NO.
I DO NOT INTEND TO KILL THE VAMPIRE KING.
NOR DO I INTEND TO LET ANYONE ELSE DO IT.
WHAT?!

THE VAMPIRE KING MUST NOT BE KILLED.
FROM NOW ON, I AM ON HIS SIDE.
PUSH

WHAT ARE YOU AFTER, BLACK SWAN?
NEGOTIATIONS ARE EASIER WITH A WEAKENED OPPONENT.
YOU INJURE ME AND THEN CALL YOURSELF MY ALLY?
IF YOU DO NOT KILL ME, THOSE HANDS WILL CONSUME YOU.
NEGOTIATIONS?
EITHER WAY, YOU HAVE NO CHOICE IN THE MATTER.
IF YOU DO NOT ACCEPT MY HELP, YOU WILL PERISH.
...I CAN'T EVEN FIGHT DHAMPIRES.
WITH THESE WOUNDS...
TO HELL WITH THAT!
ZA...

FOOM
STAND ASIDE, BLACK SWAN!
I WILL KILL HIM AND END ALL THIS...!!
I WILL NOT MOVE.
I WILL NOT LET IT END.
BA
ARE YOU MAD, BLACK SWAN?!
BA
BA
BA
IF THAT'S THE WAY YOU FEEL, I'LL JUST HAVE TO KILL YOU BOTH!!
KIIIIIIN

RRRAAAGGHH!!
AAAAAAA
VISH
YOU WOULD TURN YOUR SWORDS AGAINST ME?
JIN RENKA?

GASP
THAT FACE...

WHAT KIND OF VOW?
LIKE I SAID, TO PROTECT YOU.
OKAY... BUT I'M NOT A FRAIL PRINCESS, YOU KNOW.
AND I DON'T LIKE IT WHEN YOU GET ALL SERIOUS.
INSTEAD OF SWEARING VOWS, TRY SMILING SOMETIMES.
THAT'S ENOUGH FOR ME!
YUKI...?!

KIIIIIIIN
THUD
KLANG
AH...
AHH...

VA
WHAT IS THIS GIRL THINKING ?!
GRIT
CHNK
SURROUND THEM!
...
DON'T LET THEM ESCAPE!
ZZ
SHA

LEAP
FFFF
RAT-A-
TAT-TAT
CHK
OH NO!
I FORGOT ABOUT THE MOUN-TAIN CAT!
MMPH!
AUGH!
CHK
CHK
CHK
CHK
CAN YOU FLY, STRAUSS ?!

RAT-
-A-TAT-
-TAT-
GAGH!
YOU'RE NOT GETTING AWAY!!
SHA
OOM
?!

I CAN'T LET YOU DO THAT.
BLACK SWAN!
FOOOOOOM
AKABARA AND THE MOUNTAIN CAT ARE STILL INSIDE THE BARRIER!
BUT...
THERE'S NO WAY WE CAN CATCH THEM NOW...
THEN, PERHAPS TOMORROW?
PAT

FARE THEE WELL.
WHOOOOO
FLASH
!!
KIIIIIIIN
AUGH!!

...
THE BLACK SWAN TAKING STRAUSS'S SIDE?
HAS SHE GONE MAD?
WHOOOOO
THE RECORD OF A FALLEN VAMPIRE 1 (THE END)

THE RECORD OF A

FALLEN VAMPIRE

THANK YOU FOR READING THE *RECORD OF A FALLEN VAMPIRE.* WHEN I FIRST RECEIVED THE STORY, I REMEMBERED A POEM I HAD HEARD OVER TEN YEARS BEFORE.

"IF I CAN MEET YOU SOMEDAY, IF YOU ARE WAITING FOR ME, THEN MY LONG, LONG JOURNEY WAS NOT SO BAD AFTER ALL."

EXACTLY LIKE STRAUSS'S SEARCH FOR HIS QUEEN, ISN'T IT? WHETHER HE WILL EVER BE WITH HIS ADELHEID AGAIN IS FOR LATER IN THE STORY, BUT THE PAIN HE FEELS IS REFLECTED IN THAT POEM. NOW THAT I THINK ABOUT IT, I DIDN'T GET MUCH CHANCE TO DRAW THE CHARACTERS' BEAUTIFUL SMILES...SOME OF THESE PEOPLE ARE IN EVERY ISSUE BUT NEVER SMILE AT ALL.

"THE THOUSAND-YEAR-OLD VAMPIRE KING," "THE AMAZINGLY UNFORTUNATE GUY WHOSE GIRL WAS KILLED WITH HIS OWN SWORDS," AND "THE ANGRY GIRL"—I BELIEVE I'LL GET TO DRAW THEM SMILING SOMEDAY, AND I'D BE HONORED IF YOU STAY WITH THE SERIES TILL THEN.

-YURI KIMURA

THE RECORD
OF A FALLEN VAMPIRE

1

SPECIAL THANKS

TAKUMI TEPPEI
YUUKA NISHIOKA
HARUKA
EDITOR: NOBUAKI
YUMURA

AND TO ALL
READERS!

AUTHOR'S AFTERWORD

"LET'S DO A VAMPIRE BOOK."

IT WAS MY EDITOR WHO SUGGESTED THIS, NOT ME.

"WE HAVE THIS NEW ARTIST NAMED YURI KIMURA, AND SHE WANTS TO DO A VAMPIRE BOOK. I'D LIKE YOU TO WRITE THE STORY, SHIRODAIRA-SAN."

I'M PARAPHRASING A LITTLE, BUT THAT'S BASICALLY THE GIST OF THE CONVERSATION.

BUT I DID NOT IMMEDIATELY JUMP ON BOARD.

"UM, I WANT TO DO A MILITARY FANTASY SERIES WITH A PRETTY GIRL USING CUNNING STRATEGY TO DEFEAT AN INVINCIBLE FLYING MAGIC SUMO WRESTLER WHO'S SO POWERFUL HE CAN SINK BATTLESHIPS WITH A SINGLE SPELL. MAYBE A FEW MAGICAL GIRL POWER-UPS."

"VAMPIRES ALSO FLY, AND THEY CAN USE MAGIC."

"I GUESS..."

I THINK WE SAID SOMETHING LIKE THAT. MAYBE WE DIDN'T. BUT THIS IS HOW EDITORS AND MANGA WRITERS FIND COMMON GROUND.

PUTTING THAT ASIDE, THERE ARE AN UNBELIEVABLE NUMBER OF NOVELS, MANGA, ANIME AND MOVIES ABOUT VAMPIRES, BOTH IN THE EAST AND IN THE WEST. FROM WORLD-FAMOUS WORKS TO UNDERGROUND CULT PIECES, EVERYONE CAN IMAGINE A BASIC STORY OUTLINE WHEN THEY HEAR THE WORD VAMPIRE, WHICH IS PART OF THE REASON THEY HOLD SUCH UNIVERSAL APPEAL. HOWEVER, THIS ALSO MAKES IT REALLY DIFFICULT TO MAKE THE STORY UNIQUE.

ALSO, WHEN MY EDITOR GAVE ME THE ASSIGNMENT, THERE WAS ALREADY A VAMPIRE MANGA THAT HAD OVERWHELMING POPULAR SUPPORT, AND I KNEW IT WOULD BE HARD TO AVOID BEING NEGATIVELY COMPARED TO IT. (APPARENTLY, MY EDITOR HAD NEVER HEARD OF IT.)

TO TRY AND MAKE A VAMPIRE MANGA WITH ME AND A BRAND-NEW ARTIST DESPITE ALL THIS ONCE AGAIN DROVE HOME THAT THIS EDITOR IS WILLING TO TAKE RISKS. THE FACT THAT I TOOK ON THE JOB SAYS THE SAME ABOUT ME.

SO MY NAME IS KYO SHIRODAIRA, THE AUTHOR OF THIS BOOK. OBVIOUSLY, THIS VAMPIRE BOOK BEARS LITTLE RESEMBLANCE TO MOST VAMPIRE STORIES. THE TITLE DOES NOT HAVE ANY PARTICULARLY DEEP MEANING—WE PICKED IT AT RANDOM.

AS THE STORY PROGRESSES IT MAY BECOME MORE LIKE OTHER VAMPIRE STORIES, AND THERE ARE A FEW IDEAS I HAVE IN MIND THAT WILL TAKE IT IN THAT DIRECTION, BUT I'M NOT SURE IF I'LL USE THEM OR NOT. I'M PRETTY SURE THE MAGIC SUMO WRESTLER WON'T BE IN IT THOUGH. I'LL HAVE TO USE THAT IDEA SOMEWHERE ELSE.

THE RECORD OF A FALLEN VAMPIRE MAY HAVE LOTS OF PROBLEMS AHEAD OF IT, BUT I HOPE YOU'LL JOIN US FOR THE DURATION ANYWAY.

I PRAY WE WILL MEET AGAIN IN VOLUME TWO.

-KYO SHIRODAIRA

THE RECORD OF A FALLEN VAMPIRE
VOL. 1
VIZ MEDIA EDITION

STORY BY: KYO SHIRODAIRA ART BY: YURI KIMURA

Translation & Adaptation...**Andrew Cunningham**
Touch-up Art & Lettering...**John Hunt**
Design...**Courtney Utt**
Editor...**Amy Yu**

Editor in Chief, Books...**Alvin Lu**
Editor in Chief, Magazines...**Marc Weidenbaum**
VP of Publishing Licensing...**Rika Inouye**
VP of Sales...**Gonzalo Ferreyra**
Sr. VP of Marketing...**Liza Coppola**
Publisher...**Hyoe Narita**

Printed in the U.S.A.

Published by VIZ Media, LLC
P.O. Box 77010
San Francisco, CA 94107

10 9 8 7 6 5 4 3 2 1
First printing, May 2008

viz media
What would you pay for peace of mind?
YUMEKUI KENBUN
NIGHTMARE INSPECTOR
STORY AND ART BY SHIN MASHIBA
YUMEKUI KENBUN
NIGHTMARE INSPECTOR
Suffer from nightmares? Meet Hiruko. He's more than a special kind of private investigator—he's a dream eater. And he'll rid you of your darkest visions...but at what price?
Find out in Nightmare Inspector—MANGA ON SALE NOW!
On sale at store.viz.com
Also available at your local bookstore and comic store.
RATED T+ FOR OLDER TEEN
ratings.viz.com
VIZ MEDIA
www.viz.com
© 2002 Shin Mashiba/SQUARE ENIX